MORE
BEHAVIOR
SOLUTIONS
IN and BEYOND the
Inclusive Classroom

BETH AUNE, OTR/L
BETH BURT & PETER GENNARO

More Behavior Solutions in and Beyond the Inclusive Classroom

All marketing and publishing rights guaranteed to
and reserved by:

FUTURE HORIZONSINC.

721 W. Abram Street
Arlington, Texas 76013
800-489-0727
817-277-0727
817-277-2270 (fax)
E-mail: info@FHautism.com
www.FHautism.com

ISBN: 9781935274483

This work is dedicated to the many students whose
daily challenges and successes have inspired us.
We are privileged to share your journey.

Acknowledgments

Thank you to my grandmothers, Betty Aune and Virginia Bell, whose strength of character, steadfast faith in God and family, grace, beauty, charm, and intelligence inspired me to reach for the stars and embrace life's endless and joyful possibilities.

~ **Beth Aune**

Many thanks to all the staff at Future Horizons for all of their hard work behind the scenes. This truly is a collaboration. My contributions to this book would have never been possible without the help of many families, dedicated professionals, and educators (especially the teachers and staff at Belvedere Elementary). I am grateful to you all for your willingness to share your experiences and your lives with me, and I am awed by your determination, excitement and perseverance in changing a child's life. My love and gratitude to my wonderful family and friends. I am so incredibly blessed to have you in my life! During times of laughter, stress, tears and joy, I can always count on you. Lastly, but not least, to God, who reminds me often that He has a plan for all of our kids (Jer 29:11). We are given the privilege of being part of that plan.

For William, David, Dominic and Melina - the next generation of students.

~ **Beth Burt**

I would like to acknowledge those who made it possible for me to have received my own education when I was young: my mother, father, and sister had the foresight to realize that only with the appropriate education would I find myself in a position to choose my future. I want to further acknowledge those teachers and administrators who did more than just present curriculum, but saw within me and others a potential to perhaps create a positive difference during the short time we are here.

~ **Peter Gennaro**

Table of Contents

Introduction

Our first book, *Behavior Solutions for the Inclusive Classroom*, focused on challenging behaviors in the classroom that were commonly described by educators and were based on our direct experiences as educator, service provider, and parent. These behaviors were not limited to students with identified disabilities, but they were all identified as behaviors that impeded the learning process. Many teachers have expressed their appreciation of the direct and concise format of the book. They have also reported considerable success after implementing the strategies that we recommended. Our subsequent experiences with students, teachers, and families helped us identify behaviors beyond the classroom. We wrote this book in response to that feedback. We are pleased to be able to add to our earlier efforts and hope that you will find our second book equally useful. Once again, it is our hope that the content and format of this manual are clear and helpful. It is our goal to offer solutions that can be implemented at little or no cost and that can be learned in a short period of time.

The behaviors that surface may or may not be directly related to a known disability. You will encounter varying disabilities and degrees of disability in your career. Some of your students will come to you with a label of Autism Spectrum Disorder, Asperger's Syndrome, Tourette's Syndrome, Learning Disabled, Speech Impaired, etc. The ideas presented here are intended to be specific to behaviors you will encounter, regardless of the disability associated with them.

As in our first work, this book is divided into sections that include: (1) Inside the Classroom, (2) Outside the Classroom, (3) PE and Play, (4) Passing Periods, (5) Lunchtime and Snack, and (6) Communicating Solutions for Behavior Problems. This format offers a "snapshot" of a typical school day. We are not suggesting that all the behaviors you will encounter can neatly be categorized into "sections," but it is our hope that you can use the organization of the sections and chapter titles to find ideas and solutions quickly.

Section One

Inside the Classroom

The task facing teachers today centers on much more than the delivery of curriculum and instruction. Today's teachers must also focus on the successful shaping of student behaviors in and out of the classroom. In our opening chapters, we touch on some of the behaviors a student can demonstrate in a classroom that make the daily task of a teacher more difficult. As these behaviors are brought under control or minimized, the learning potential of all students in the classroom can be maximized. Identifying and implementing strategies to address problematic behavior will result in a more optimal learning environment for both students and teachers.

Leaving the Classroom without Permission

Leaving the classroom without permission can disrupt the learning process for students and it can be a safety issue. A student may sneak out when your back is turned or bolt suddenly out the door. There are a variety of reasons, which may include:

- Lack of awareness of the need to ask permission to leave
- Flight response to an anxiety or sensory issue
- Avoidance of class work or of a situation

The first priority is to alert administration immediately if you can't find the student within a few minutes. The adult who locates the child will need to assess the situation. Is the student ready to return to the classroom?

Solutions!

- Engage the student in class work when he or she returns to class. <u>Do not welcome them back with either a hug or a lecture.</u>

- Talk with the student later and make a plan to prevent similar instances. Check for understanding of the situation. "Johnny, tell me again why you left the room today?" Address the situation by making it clear to the student that leaving the classroom without permission is not allowed. Offer a concrete plan such as, "Next time you have to leave the classroom, you need to raise your hand and wait for permission."

- Develop visual supports (See Appendix A) to help the student remember what behavior is expected.

- Set up a "safe" area of the classroom where the student can go when she is upset.

- Allow the student to take a break in a pre-determined quiet location or take a walk to prepare him to return to class.

Lack of Focus in Whole Group Instruction

Some students will be more attentive in a small group where they can receive more direct instruction. However, most teachers need to instruct the whole group, which is especially true as students get older. Many students have language-processing deficits. Some students tend to lose interest quickly, especially when less attention is paid to them directly. If they begin to drift off and lose focus, they may draw other students off task as well and slow the learning process for themselves and others.

Solutions!

- Begin the lesson by asking the student a question that will draw him into the main idea of what will be discussed in the whole group. This personal connection can help the student be more interested and engaged.

- Call on the student often to keep him interested, and ask him questions about which you know he has background knowledge.

- Give the student a specific task that requires him to be regularly engaged. Set up a plan with the student to ask one question relevant to the topic each class period.

- Seat the student in a preferred location in front of or near other students who pay attention.

Behavior?

Out-of-Seat Behavior

Today, more than ever, educators are faced with teaching core subjects for longer periods to prepare the class to master state standards. This requires the students to sit at their desks for long periods, and they may lose focus. Many students may have challenges with sustained sitting and have a sensory need for movement to help them maintain an alert state. The student may leave his seat to pace, invent reasons to get up (sharpen pencils, get a drink of water, get some tissue), or stand up at his desk.

Solutions!

- Schedule movement breaks (see Appendix B) for the entire class inside the classroom, such as standing to "stretch and wiggle."

- Allow the student to help pass out papers, clean the board, or assist the teacher with technical media.

- Let the student stand at the back or perimeter of the classroom or at his desk.

- Allow a very motor-restless student to have a movement break outside the classroom. See Appendix B.

- Use oral strategies. When the mouth is kept busy, often the body will feel calmer and the student can sit still. See Appendix C.

- Provide hand fidget tools, such as Koosh balls, rubber bands, paper clips, and tangles.

In-Seat Behavior

Some students have an increased need for movement owing to their sensory profile. They may engage in humming, tapping a pencil, shifting position frequently, and appearing distracted. It is important to identify if the student's behavior is interfering with the others' learning. Sometimes, a teacher is the one who is distracted. Keep in mind that this student may be engaging in some sensory strategies to help him pay attention to the teacher's instruction.

Solutions!

- Place the student in an area of the classroom where he does not distract the teacher or classmates.

- Provide alternative fidget tools that are less noticeable, such as items to keep in his pocket or ones that do not make noise.

- Let the student keep a hard candy in his mouth to reduce mouth noises.

- Ask the student questions more frequently to ensure he is paying attention. Some children may appear distracted, but they may actually be attending.

- Allow the student to stand at his desk when he needs to.

Behavior?

Difficulty Completing Independent Work

Some students have poor motor skills, decreased organizational skills, and challenges with task sequencing. They may have difficulty with language processing and handwriting, or they may be distracted by environmental stimuli. This student doesn't have materials ready, can be slow to start an assignment, can appear distracted or disorganized, and can be frustrated or oppositional.

Solutions!

- Identify a consistent location to keep materials secure and readily available, such as a container attached to the side of the desk or on the floor. For example, some students may benefit from attaching pencils to the desk with Velcro.

- Ensure that the student understands the intent of the assignment and make sure he starts it correctly. Don't wait until he is halfway through to offer guidance.

- Modify lengthy assignments to a manageable level.

- Reward efforts to stay on task (e.g. verbal praise, a token economy).

- Allow the student to wear headphones or earplugs during pencil-and-paper activities.

Meltdown

First, let's talk about our definition of a "meltdown." This chapter uses "meltdown" and "tantrum" interchangeably. It can be a result of unmanaged frustration, or it can appear out of nowhere. Observable behavior may include crying, kicking, screaming, hitting, throwing objects, biting, banging the head onto the wall or floor, collapsing to the floor, name-calling, etc. This can last from a few minutes to over an hour.

We are not going to pretend that there is a magic formula that we can give you to guide your actions during meltdown or crisis. Thus, it is imperative that the adults in the situation have insight into the causes of a student's behavior.

Solutions!

- First, ensure that the teacher, student, and others are safe.

- Remove hazards from the environment.

- Call for additional adult assistance.

- Maintain a calm voice and demeanor and keep talking to a minimum.

- Once the child has begun to calm down, you might offer rhythmical and closed-ended strategies, such as rocking, drinking water, counting, spelling, deep breathing, and singing.

This challenging behavior may require additional and ongoing support from your site psychologist or behavior specialist.

Difficulty Organizing Materials

Many students have poor motor planning and sequencing skills. Often, their visual system is under-responsive, and it does not organize sensory input well. These students have extreme difficulty making a plan to organize materials, and they also often have decreased fine motor skills. Messy backpacks overflow with extra papers, desk drawers are chaotic, utensils are unusable or missing, and papers are not put in binders.

Solutions!

- Replace the three-ring binder with a flexed file folder (the accordion type). This reduces the organizational steps that are needed with a three-ring binder to a much simpler filing method for papers. It also allows the student to see the entire folder at a glance.

- Prompt him to organize papers or throw away the old ones at the end of the day when he is packing his backpack.

- Remind him to take inventory and clean out his pencil box on a scheduled basis.

- Have a peer help him clean and organize his desk each week. Reduce the level of assistance to modeling as independence increases.

- Provide containers to attach to the sides of his desk. This will let the student see the contents easily versus having to bend and peer into a dark desk.

Classroom Celebrations

Although special events such as birthday and holiday parties can be fun, they can also be overwhelming and chaotic for some students. The routine is different, new people may be in the classroom, different foods and odors can be confusing, and the social expectations change from the customary.

Solutions!

- Give the parent and student advance notice to help with their expectations.

- Use social stories.

- Include the student in the party preparation. This gives him concrete information and extra time to prepare.

- If the student is on a special diet (e.g. Gluten Free/ Casein Free), have alternative snacks sent in so the student doesn't feel left out.

- Encourage, but don't force, the student to participate. Expect this student to need to take a break from the stimulation.

- Have a back-up plan if the student becomes extremely overwhelmed. He may need to go to another classroom or designated "safe" area on campus.

Notes

Outside the Classroom

Many of the students described in this book have a need for predictability and may have difficulty with the concept of time. When things change, they can feel out of control and unsure of what is going to happen next, and this may result in confusion or a discipline issue. Think how many times a day a student transitions—waking up in the morning, getting ready for school, traveling to school, arriving to school, etc. In each of these tasks, there may be even more unexpected change—perhaps the child's favorite cereal is gone, or his favorite shirt is in the laundry. Maybe there is a new bus driver or a new bus route. Even classes that we think of as fun or enjoyable, like music or art, can bring unexpected transitions and challenges. For these students, the standard verbal warning may not be enough to prepare them for transitioning. This section provides some helpful suggestions for these common behaviors.

Riding the Bus

Many students enjoy the experience of riding the bus, but some find it difficult. They may leave their seats, appear agitated, be disruptive, cover their ears, or become anxious.

Solutions!

- Provide something familiar to occupy the student, such as a portable music or video device, book, or toy.

- Give him a closed-ended task or game to play with another student (familiar car games, such as counting types/colors, looking for different state license plates, etc.). The teacher can be prepared to ask the students about their experience.

- Seat the student near the bus driver.

Getting Off the Bus and Out of the Car

This can be a challenging time for students because they may be going into a situation they perceive as fearful. A student who has trouble with this transition may refuse to get off the bus or out of the parent's car or come out crying and uncooperative. Students are often more willing to make a transition when it is to something preferential, so it is important to help them experience exiting the bus or car as something positive, right from the start.

Solutions!

- Identify his favorite person (student, teacher, etc.) and have this person meet the student when he arrives at school, possibly with a tangible reward.

- Have a preferred and familiar person walk onto the bus and assist the student with this transition.

- Have the parents and teachers work together to arrange for the student to deliver an item to the classroom. This acts as a good transition object.

- Allow younger students to borrow a toy from the classroom the day before. They will be excited about bringing it back the next day to play with it.

Pull-Out Services

Many students in the general education classroom spend part of their day outside of class to partake in various supportive services from other school professionals, such as a special education teacher (direct or pull-out), speech therapist, occupational therapist, Adapted Physical Education specialist, physical therapist, or behaviorist. While the general education teacher may have been exposed to strategies to help these students, other service providers may not have had that opportunity and may struggle with understanding the behaviors. Some students have difficulty making transitions from the classroom to the pull-out service location and may exhibit other challenging behaviors with the specialists, including decreased attending, motor restlessness, and anxiety.

Solutions!

- Verbally prepare the student for the transition.

- Provide a daily visual schedule (see Appendix A) to remind the student of the day's events.

- Share the strategies that have been found to be effective with the various service providers.

- If the child is using a positive behavior support, such as token economy, it should travel with the student outside of class.

Behavior?

End of the School Day

Many special needs students are not as effective at being aware of the daily schedule at school as compared with their peers. They do not always "tune in" to the environmental cues that are available to them to help them prepare for the end of the school day. This student does not alert to the built-in cues in the classroom, such as the teacher's instructions to get ready to leave, the time on the clock, and peers readying for dismissal. When it is time to leave, they are often disorganized and may become anxious.

Solutions!

- Alert the student to the clock and remind him that the time is nearing dismissal.

- Use more frequent reminders to prepare the student to leave.

- Give the student additional time to gather belongings.

- Provide the student with a checklist to ensure that he has his homework assignments, parent communication, and belongings packed in his backpack. Review the checklist with him.

- Enlist a peer to assist the student.

- Ask a parent or a specialist (such as an occupational therapist) to come into the class at the beginning of the year to teach this process, and then this support can be phased out.

Behavior?

Art

There are many sensory issues related to art that students with special needs face. Some may have tactile defensiveness. Others may show excessive sensory-seeking behaviors, exploring the materials with their hands and mouths. Many students lack fine motor skills, so art is a difficult subject. They may also often have problems coming up with an idea for a creative project. These students can tantrum when required to use materials such as finger paints, glue, or papier-mâché; they may exhibit shutdown or avoidance; and they can be extremely messy or play with the art media inappropriately (e.g. painting their own hands, arms, or face).

Solutions!

- Allow the tactile-defensive child to wear surgical gloves to keep his hands clean.

- Let him use a paintbrush to apply glue.

- Explore art activities that are more technical and concrete in nature, such as computer animation or photography.

- Help the student organize his work area.

- Reduce the amount of materials by providing *only* the amount that is necessary to help with organization.

- Demonstrate and explain the appropriate way to use the art supplies. Don't expect the student to figure it out simply by observing.

- Remember that it is very difficult for some students to stop a project at the end of class before it is completed. Try giving several verbal warnings or give them a directive, such as, "color one more flower." Remind them when the next day for art is scheduled.

- Be prepared to offer an alternative assignment if the original one is too difficult or if the student works too quickly.

Music

While music class can be a great opportunity for many students to sing and learn to play instruments, it can cause stress and anxiety in others and possibly lead to a meltdown or other unwanted behavior. The sound of certain instruments, certain notes, hearing more than one instrument or voice at time, and the unpredictability of another student playing a loud instrument can be triggers for unwanted behavior. On the other hand, there has been anecdotal evidence that music and singing have improved language development and self-expression. It is important to encourage participation, while being aware of the challenges that the special needs student has with music class.

Solutions!

- Provide a visual agenda (Appendix A) to review at the beginning of the school day to prepare the student for the day's schedule.

- Review the schedule for music class to further alleviate anxiety or confusion for the student.

- Be direct, calm, clear, and as concrete as possible with verbal instruction and guidance.

- Be clear about the rules, and review the rules and structure of the class. For example, are there assigned places for students to stand to await instruction or should they begin to warm up as soon as they enter the room for chorus or band?

- Look for a way to reward participation.

- Allow the student to move around or take a break during class if he appears to be frustrated, confused, or over-stimulated.

Computer Lab

For most students, the occasional journey out of homeroom can be a welcome change of scenery. Most classes will spend a particular amount of time in the school computer lab each week. However, the change in routine, having less structure, and increased expectation for independent work, as well as a higher student-to-teacher ratio, can lead to behavioral challenges for special needs students. They may have difficulty starting and staying on task, sitting still, asking for help, or using headphones.

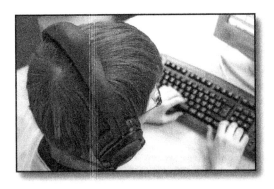

Solutions!

- Prepare the student for the change in routine.

- Remind the student of the behavioral expectations and assignment for the computer lab before he goes. The teacher may also need to review those expectations during that class period.

- Share successful strategies (e.g. visual supports, positive reinforcement/rewards) with the computer teacher or technician and ask them to use these strategies.

- Help the student choose a seat and computer that he can use every time he goes to lab. This will provide added structure and a sense of predictability.

- Be flexible and allow the student to work on other computer programs that are of more interest to encourage participation or act as a reward for participating in less-preferred assignments.

- Provide closer and more frequent supervision to ensure participation and understanding.

Library

The library has a unique set of rules for students. They are required to be very quiet, and they need to listen to a read-aloud story while sitting still on the carpet. Often, a student is required to check out books only at his identified reading level or by theme or subject. Tantrums, using a loud voice, wiggling on the carpet, touching other students, and difficulty choosing a book are some of the behaviors that special needs students may exhibit.

Solutions!

- Teach the child to whisper. Simply saying "Be quiet" does not provide enough concrete information. Practice whispering with him and praise him for doing so.

- Provide a chair for the student to sit in to help him identify his place on the floor and decrease bumping other students.

- Give the student additional time, if needed, to navigate the book checkout process and avoid the confusion of being jostled in a mass of bodies.

- Help the student alert to the teacher's non-verbal signal for "be quiet."

- Read a social story about library behavior to the student before leaving homeroom.

Notes

PE and Play

This section focuses on PE, which is a structured activity directed by an adult, and the relatively unstructured recess time. In both instances, our students are faced with the demands of participating in a larger group as compared to the relative order of the classroom. Paying attention to and following a teacher's or playground supervisor's directions, understanding the social requirements, and dealing with a poor sensory awareness and lacking motor skills are all examples of challenges that students face. This section provides specific examples of these challenges and offers some helpful suggestions.

PE

Some special needs students have difficulty with the motor skills necessary for PE. They may lack organization, have poor time management, or have challenges changing from school to PE clothes. Others lack the social skills or confidence necessary for team sports. They may have difficulty understanding and following the rules of the game; they can be overly rigid during team sports and have difficulty engaging in competitive games; they may act out or withdraw. Much like Computer Lab or the Library, PE tends to be a setting with a very different structure and set of rules. Even though PE teachers may be very skilled, they are usually working with much larger groups of students, often with little or no assistance. PE can be among the most difficult times for students who have trouble with large groups and situations where the rules change often.

Solutions!

- If students change clothes for PE, have special needs students change five minutes prior to the other students.

- Adapt the rules to be very simple and basic.

- Modify the space in the gym into smaller areas for students who have difficulty with large spaces.

- Provide physical assistance to help special needs students understand terms such as "throw," "catch," "kick," etc.

- Help the student identify the goal in each sport—it could be simply running with the team.

- When teams are divided, be sure that the student is included and paired with a peer model.

- Explain, perhaps through videos, pictures, or social stories, the concept of working as a team.

- Instead of competition, teach physical fitness through the use of fitness machines, such as treadmills, stair steppers, and weights.

Unsafe or Inappropriate Use of Equipment

Many special needs students are "sensory seeking" children who crave and require excessive movement and the sensation of bumping, jumping, and crashing. They may use the equipment on the playground or during PE in unsafe ways, such as jumping off high platforms on jungle gyms, swinging very high and jumping off onto the ground, climbing up slides or going down them on their stomachs, or hanging upside down on the monkey bars. These children can be a danger to themselves and to other students.

Solutions!

- Take the student to the playground by himself and practice safe use of the equipment. Initially, he may require several demonstrations and will need to review the safety rules periodically.

- Before each recess, have him read a written list of the rules that he worked with an adult to prepare. Writing the rules and hearing his own voice will be more meaningful than simply listening to his teacher.

- Pair the student with a peer who can be a good role model for safe playground behavior.

- Review the student's performance after recess to give him immediate feedback. Positively reinforce appropriate behavior to encourage repetition (e.g. a token economy, verbal praise, or a meaningful privilege).

- Make sure that the playground supervisor is aware of the student who can be unsafe so he or she can keep a closer eye on him.

- Provide additional adult supervision (e.g. special education aides or teacher's assistants).

"Aggressive" Behavior on the Playground or During PE

Although there can be some children who are intentionally aggressive, many students who are labeled "aggressive" often lack awareness of the force behind their movement, or they have challenges controlling their momentum. They throw and kick balls too hard, may lack awareness of their body's position in space, and appear uncoordinated. Some students have difficulty modulating their physical responses to playground activities. They may begin playing calmly, but then they become overly aroused and begin to play roughly or seem to lack self-control. Other children may be defensive to unexpected touch (tactile defensive) on the playground or while waiting in line and exhibit a "fight response" by hitting other students.

Solutions!

● Be aware of signals that indicate over-arousal, such as a loud voice and quick or undirected movements. Suggest a "cool down" break before the behavior escalates.

● Position the tactile-defensive student at the end of the line where he is less likely to be bumped.

● Allow him to gather materials after the crowd of students has dispersed to reduce the potential for unexpected and uncomfortable touch.

● Have him sit or stand at the perimeter of the group during games and activities.

● This student may require support from an occupational therapist, who can work to teach him to be more aware of his position in space and the force behind his movement.

Difficulty Joining in Group Activities/Isolating

Part of the process of social growth occurs in non-academic settings. We are speaking specifically of the playground or sports fields. Recess for young students can often be trying and frustrating. Inappropriate behaviors often occur prior to those times when students must leave the relative security of the classroom and enter the "outside" realm; they feel stress due to anticipation. When these students attempt to include themselves in peer activities, they are often awkward and find limited success. They may resort to self-isolation, as this is more predictable and comfortable. However, some isolation can be restorative and self-regulating and should be allowed or encouraged.

Solutions!

- Use social stories to help the student prepare for what to expect. If the student knows to expect occasional rejection, he may not be so fast to give up an attempt to be included. Social stories and conversation with the student will also help him learn how to identify those student groups he could to try to join, as well as those he should avoid.

- Provide guidance to deal with bullying. Teach strategies to avoid negative situations and seek out appropriate peers.

- Allow student groups to join the teacher in the classroom at lunch or recess to work on non-academic activities, such as games or crafts, in a more structured and less threatening environment. These can be good opportunities to foster social connections through shared interests. These connections can generalize to outdoor activities.

- Don't demand or expect the student's 100% participation.

- Work with the student's family and other team members to identify appropriate expectations for a healthy combination of social inclusion and restorative private time.

Challenges with Turn-Taking

One of most important characteristics of maintaining friendships is a student's ability to take turns. Whether in a board game or an outdoor sport, this act of cooperation can often be a difficult concept for special needs students to master. Often, they may not come to school with much experience in this area, especially if they have no siblings or if they have not had opportunities to practice this skill.

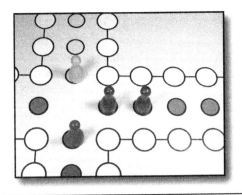

Solutions!

- Simplify the process as much as possible. Choose games or activities that are short in length and end relatively quickly, such as tic-tac-toe.

- For a drawing activity, try pairing the student with an older student who can act as a model and a guide. In this activity, one student puts something in the drawing and then the other student puts in something else, and so on until the drawing is completed. This is a concrete way to teach turn-taking.

- Generalize success in short-term games and activities to longer and longer periods of time, with more complex games and activities.

- Help the student organize his work area.

- Have an older special needs student work with a group of younger students to teach them how to take turns in a game or activity. Oftentimes, it is less a lack of understanding than an impulsive or self-centered action that causes trouble in this area. Using this "We teach best what we need to learn" idea can help students develop an understanding of the rules of turn-taking, as well as build their self-confidence by helping younger students.

Behavior?

Being a Poor Sport

Many special needs students have significant challenges with participating in games that have a winner and a loser. They toss board games off tables, kick balls away from the group, or engage in name-calling. These students may eventually become disengaged and avoid participation in competitive games. Quitting a game if he is behind, throwing a tantrum if he loses a game, or being overly controlling and bossy are behaviors that result from rigid and concrete thinking, decreased awareness of the game's structure, perfectionism, or anxiety.

Solutions!

- Try playing team games in class and point out that "sometimes we win and sometimes we lose, and that is okay."

- Review the concept of being a "good sport" using concrete examples. Many of our students have difficulty understanding an abstract concept like being a "good sport."

- Set up opportunities to practice losing games and reward the absence of negative behaviors.

- Teach the concept of being a "good sport" when the student wins a game in addition to when he loses one. This will give him an opportunity to practice sportsmanship when he is more willing to listen and learn.

- Point out and give attention to peers who lose gracefully. Sometimes our students have difficulty with perspective-taking and are not aware that other students also lose games but manage their disappointment well.

Notes

Passing Periods

*W*e define "passing periods" as the times a student moves from one setting to another, either with his class or separately. As any teacher will tell you, the behavior a student demonstrates outside the classroom can also have an effect on his learning and success. The chapters in this section focus on the less structured transition times in a student's day. Behaviors that begin during these times can carry over into the classroom. Being aware of and prepared for these situations can minimize negative behaviors and optimize learning opportunities.

Behavior?

Getting in Line

Lining up before transitions is a skill that is introduced as early as preschool, and it occurs often. However, some students have difficulty mastering this requirement, despite the numerous opportunities to learn it. They may initially line up but not remain in line; push, poke, or shove other students while in line; or not get into the line of students at all. This may occur for a variety of reasons: standing still in one place for an extended period is hard for the active student, keeping hands to oneself is difficult for the sensory-seeking student, and others may simply not notice the cues that it is time to line up.

Solutions!

- Don't make special needs students wait too long: send part of the group out of the classroom rather than have them wait for the entire group to line up.

- Focus on validating the appropriate behavior of lining up, rather than upon the negative behavior of leaving the line.

- Assign the student a consistently designated position in line. This student may need to line up last, not only to emphasize the visual cue that there is a line forming, but also to reduce waiting time.

- Have the motor-restless child who has challenges controlling his body act as the door holder. This gives him a specific job to do with his body and hands.

Behavior?

Staying with the Group

One of the recurring themes of this book is the idea that when the typical structure of a classroom changes to a transition, a student's unwanted behavior is more likely to surface. Passing periods from one class to another are prime examples of a time this can occur. In these times, students often find it difficult to remain with the group to which they are assigned. Wandering off and disrupting others are some of the behaviors that can result from having challenges with making transitions.

Solutions!

- Give the student a specific task while moving with the group. He could be in charge of carrying books or other materials needed for the new location.

- Place the student in the front or the back of the line with the task of leading the group in the front or keeping the group in line from the back.

- Create the possibility of a tangible reward. If the group is going to the library, for instance, the student may have first choice of books if he remains with the group at all times.

- Stay as close to the student as possible. Your proximity may, in itself, be a reminder to stay with the group.

- Create a social story centered on the importance and safety issues associated with remaining with the group during transition times.

Getting to Class on Time

As discussed before, some of our students have sensory challenges or anxiety issues that make them want to avoid crowds. Many classes have as many as 30-40 students pouring into a classroom all at once; this is perceived as crowded to most of us, and even more so to the students who are easily overwhelmed by the stimulation.

Solutions!

● Develop and review social stories with special needs students about what they need to do when moving through hallways. This will help identify the stressful components and validate their emotional reactions.

● Help special needs students find a less congested path or route to get from one place to another on campus. Practice this with them until they feel more secure.

● Understand that some students may require additional time to transition from one location to another and may benefit from leaving class earlier (or later) when hallways are less congested.

● Modify the typical consequences for getting to class late.

Restroom Issues

Restrooms can be a safe haven from the commotion of a classroom or a hallway, or they can be a source of anxiety and avoidance. Some students use them as a tool to recover from sensory overload; but they may also use them to avoid class work. Some of the behaviors that occur include staying too long in the bathroom, covering the ears when the toilets flush, peeking under stalls at other students, removing clothing before toileting, or refusing to use the restroom all day.

Solutions!

- If a special needs student requests to go to the washroom multiple times throughout the day, determine if there is a medical condition. This student may need special permission to use the restroom more often than his peers.

- Develop a strategy and schedule to identify when he is allowed to use the restroom if he is using washroom trips (either consciously or unconsciously) as a strategy for avoiding schoolwork or other non-preferred activities.

- Identify privacy and social rules for the behavior specific to the restroom.

- Allow special needs students to use the restroom when no or few other students are there to reduce the auditory, tactile, and visual stimuli.

- Give the student access to a small restroom, such as a staff restroom or one in the nurse's station.

Notes

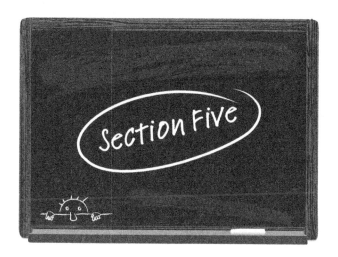

Lunchtime and Snack

*L*unchtime and snack time are situations during the school day that cause difficulties that can be overlooked easily or underreported, because the students are in large groups with a higher student-to-adult ratio. This section addresses common social, motor, and sensory challenges that students exhibit and offers some practical solutions.

Behavior?

Messy Eater

The student who eats quickly or sloppily or ends up with food on his face, hands, and clothing is at risk of social ridicule. He may have poor fine motor skills for utensil use, have difficulty in the pacing of chewing and swallowing, overstuff his mouth with food, or be unaware of the sensation of food on his hands or face.

Solutions!

● Make sure to provide special needs students with typical, heavier metal utensils, which are easier to manage than plastic; they provide additional sensory feedback and promote hand skills for eating.

● Consider offering finger foods as alternatives to messy foods, such as spaghetti.

● Provide a wet wipe rather than a flimsy paper napkin to enable the student to wash his hands and face more easily between bites and after eating.

● Encourage the student to use the restroom after lunch and a snack and teach him to use the mirror to see if his face is clean.

Behavior?

Avoids Group at Snack and Lunch

In our society, eating is a social event, but some students are overwhelmed by the crowds of students, noise, and/or the variety of smells in the cafeteria. This student becomes anxious and avoidant and may want to eat and leave quickly, or he may even refuse to enter the cafeteria.

Solutions!

- Allow the special needs student to eat in another supervised location, such as the office, resource room, classroom, or outside area if the sensory stimuli are too overwhelming.

- Assign a task or activity to help him stay occupied in a functional way if he eats quickly and needs to wait for his class.

- Let the student sit at a table near the door where odors and other stimuli are less overwhelming.

- Allow the student to sit at the perimeter of the cafeteria or at the end of the row of classmates.

- Provide this student with extra monitoring and encouragement to finish his food.

Managing Trays and Packaging

Walking through the cafeteria line, paying for food, loading the tray, finding a place to sit, and managing a variety of containers is often an overwhelming sequence of events for special needs students. In addition, many of these students have poor motor planning and lack the fine motor skills needed to carry trays and open containers. These issues can affect the child emotionally, socially, and nutritionally. They may appear avoidant, anxious, and frustrated and eat more slowly or quickly than their peers.

Solutions!

- Allow the student to line up first or last to go through the food line.

- Help the student identify a consistent place to sit. Often, having the student sit at a table closest to a wall or center aisle helps the student carry his tray in a less congested area and decreases the possibility of dropping it.

- Provide a sturdier tray (restaurant/cafeteria-style) as a simple alternative to the customary, flimsy types found in many schools.

- Encourage the student to ask for help in opening difficult containers, such as milk pouches.

Notes

Section Six

Communicating
Solutions for
Behavior Problems

*O*ur final chapters focus on the necessity for frequent and open communication among team members. If all team members are aware of the needs and progress of a student, it becomes much easier to make adjustments to his program. It is often during these times of communication that one team member can share the solutions that have proven successful with the others. It is also a way to make certain that what is expected of the student is consistent through all environments. As an educator, you know that communication is also the key to building a relationship of trust and confidence within the team, and we see the case manager as the center of this communication.

Open communication depends on our ability to report objectively on the successes the student is having, as well as the difficulties. All trusting relationships can withstand tough times, and, therefore, it is acceptable to communicate comprehensive, clear, and concise information.

Remember, not all students with IEPs require extensive communication. The IEP meetings, regular IEP grading periods, and typical communication patterns are often sufficient for most students on IEPs.

Communication Strategies for Special Ed Case Managers

Regardless of the student's educational setting, the communication will be initiated or received by the special education case manager. Many lines of communication will exist (administrator, teacher, parent, service provider), but the special education case manager should be involved in all correspondence. This can be complex, and some case managers may struggle with maintaining contact with all of these interested parties.

Solutions!

- Encourage all parties (administrator, general and special education teacher, parent, service provider) to contact the case manager on a regular basis to be part of the communication loop. For example: The general education teacher should make a point of including the special education case manager in all communications by making periodic copies of communication logs and by discussing the progress of the student on a regular basis.

- Assume personal responsibility for communication, so that all team members will have the most up-to-date information on the student's progress.

- Set aside 30-60 minutes per week to update communication with team members.

Communication Strategies for Administration

One of the most underestimated lines of communication is that between the site administrator(s) and the parent(s). To ensure thorough and effective communication, there is no substitute for having the educational leader(s) directly involved with a student's educational plan.

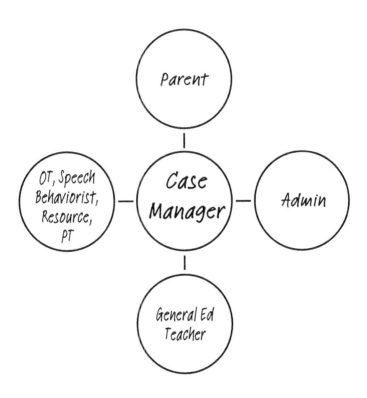

Solutions!

- Be at the IEP meetings if possible, particularly the ones that you know will focus on difficult behavior. As the educational leader on the site, the administrator's presence is an indication to the parent and the teachers that you are taking an active role in the improved behavior of the student.

- Be available, open-minded, and supportive of these kiddos. This is as equally important to the special needs student as it is to the staff.

- Consider providing the parents with additional contact information, such as your cell phone number, to use during vital situations that may occur apart from regularly scheduled meetings.

Communication Strategies for General Education Teachers

There is no more important partnership in education than that of the teacher and the parent. Communication between these two parties can often make the difference between behavior that has potential for continuous improvement and behavior that may end in steady decline. The key for general education teachers and special education case managers is to be able to communicate consistently and meaningfully, while at the same time not making it a paperwork nightmare or a series of numerous phone calls.

As a teacher of a general education classroom, you may have already established a communication system between school and home. You may find that certain parents of special needs children will request more frequent and detailed accounting of the student's day. Often, this helps parents determine if certain treatment strategies they are implementing outside of school are effective or helps them identify problem areas. Many special needs students have trouble communicating or recalling what happened during the school day, so alternative forms of communication can be designed and implemented.

Solutions!

- Regular communication through take-home checklists is an effective way to give meaningful information to a parent while not getting bogged down in writing long narratives. Appendix D is an example of such a checklist. It covers aspects of the student's day, including behavior, participation, and academic progress. It can be completed in a couple of minutes, and it affords the parent the opportunity to write back with questions or concerns.

- If appropriate, and the student is old enough, have him participate by filling out portions of the communication log. This is an effective means for the student to self-regulate.

- Contact the parent occasionally by telephone. Most parents are more than willing to have these conversations, and if you are diligent about communication from the outset, you are more than likely going to build up a level of trust with the parent that will pay dividends.

- Don't wait until there is a problem. Work closely with the parent from the beginning of your involvement with the student.

● Gather and use input from other service providers periodically (speech therapist, occupational therapist, behaviorist, etc.).

● Establish clear guidelines on how often (daily/weekly) the communication should occur and who will be responsible (teacher/instructional assistant/student) for initiating and tracking the communication.

● Agree upon specific behaviors that can be measured and what scale will be used.

● Determine, with the parent, the main concerns (trouble with homework, having a bad morning, etc.) and identify a consistent method of communication (e-mail, telephone, communication log, etc.).

Behavior?

Communication Strategies for DIS Providers

It is likely that some of the students with IEPs with whom you will work will also have DIS services (Designated Instructional Service), along with special education case management. We are referring to services such as speech and language, occupational therapy, and behavioral intervention services. It is important that these service providers be part of the regular communication process. Time constraints do not always make this easy to accomplish, but as we have said, consistent and objective communication between team members can often save hours of work in the future.

Solutions!

- Schedule a time to meet weekly with the case manager and DIS providers. This may require only five to ten minutes, but this time can be used to share information on the progress of a student and exchange successes and challenges.

- Use district e-mail to communicate with other team members and parents to exchange information.

- Always be objective and respectful toward the student while communicating with team members, even during trying times.

Notes

Visual Supports

Visual supports are pictures, written scripts, or instruction cards with pictures and/or short written directions, such as Power Cards. These supports include daily schedules, mini-schedules, activity checklists, calendars, choice boards, and picture aids, depending on the needs and age of the student. This strategy can be used to provide information, establish rules for behavior, give directions, illustrate what choices are available, prepare students for what comes next, and provide a timetable or expectations that will make the day more predictable and structured. It can also provide strategies for organizing the environment, such as labeling objects and containers.

Solutions!

- **Power Cards** – A characteristic common in children with Autism Spectrum Disorder is having a special interest that is all-consuming, such as dinosaurs, NASCAR, horses, or a favorite television show or video game. Power Cards are a visual aid that incorporates the student's special interest to teach and reinforce appropriate social interactions, including routines, behavioral expectations, and social skills. A Power Card consists of an index card or small-sized paper with a short scenario that describes how to solve a problem by using a picture of their special interest. It can be used to help a student understand his or her expectations, clarify choices, teach cause and effect between a specific behavior and its consequence, teach another's perspective, aid in generalization, or serve as a visual reminder of appropriate behavioral expectations in a given situation. It is a positive strategy that is often entertaining, as well as inexpensive and simple to develop (Autism Spectrum Institute at Illinois State University, 2011).

Sergeant Joe says, "Get to work, soldier!"	

● **Social Stories™** – Created by Carol Gray, Social Stories™ are text or stories that describe a specific social situation. They are visual cues written at the child's functioning level and individualized so that the child may reflect on the desired behavior. Included in a story is "who" is involved, "what" happens, "when" the event takes place, "why" it happens, and "how" it happens (Gray, 2000; Swaggart et al., 1995). The story sequences, explains, and sometimes illustrates social rules or concepts.

● **Visual Schedules** – These are written or picture schedules that are used to organize and structure daily activities. They may be a simple activity list that you write on the board or a laminated schedule the student can take with him or her throughout the day. Schedules can be created by using Microsoft Word or Excel and laminated so that the student can reuse them. Clip Art can make the schedule more colorful and easier to read; however, some students may not realize that showing a picture of a lunchbox doesn't mean you have to eat from a lunchbox every day (and that they can buy lunch instead).

Example of a Visual Schedule

Johnny's Monday Schedule

Time		Activity	✔ When Done
8:00 am – 8:15 am		Flag Salute, morning work, turn in homework	
8:15 am –10:00 am		Reading/Language Arts	
10:00 am –10:15 am		Recess	
10:15 am –11:15 am		Math	
11:15 am – 12:00 pm		Lunch and recess	
12:00 pm – 12:45 pm		Math	
12:45 pm – 1:00 pm		Recess	
1:00 pm – 1:30 pm		Library	
1:30 pm – 2:15 pm		Social Studies	
2:15 pm –2:30 pm		Clean up, independent reading, Time to leave	

Movement Breaks Inside and Outside the Classroom

Movement breaks that are structured throughout the day should be implemented proactively, as well as in response to a student's challenges with sitting still and attending. Consult with your district's occupational therapist for guidance in implementing these and other helpful strategies:

Solutions!

- Stand upright at the desk

- Pass out papers

- Wipe the board

- Sharpen pencils

- Put materials away

- Organize, staple, or hole-punch papers

- Do isometric exercises, such as hand-clasps or seat/desk/wall push-ups

- Use hand fidget tools

- Run an errand

- Help the custodian with chores

- Get a drink of water

- Go for a walk

- Go to the playground with supervision

Oral Sensory Strategies

Many teachers and administrators are unaware of how beneficial oral strategies can be for the student who has difficulty sitting still and paying attention. The mouth is a very regulatory part of the body (think of an infant who needs to suck to calm or an adult who chews gum or sucks on a mint). Use of the mouth helps us attain and maintain a calm, alert, and attentive state. While your school may have rules against food in the classroom, it is our experience that being flexible will result in a calmer, quieter, less disruptive, and more attentive student. The following items can be experimented with in the classroom:

Solutions!

- Straws

- Water bottles

- Hard candies, such as Jolly Ranchers

- Chewy foods, such as beef jerky, Tootsie Rolls, and licorice

- Crunchy foods, such as popcorn, chips, and granola

- Gum (e.g. Bazooka)

Oral aids such as these can be implemented during an activity, and you can ask parents to provide these types of foods/aids for snacks and lunches.

Home-School
Communication
Log Sample

Sam's Day

Date: _____

Notes from home:_____

	Followed Directions	Participated in Class	Stayed on Task	Transitions
Circle Time				
Language Arts				
Reading				
Recess				
Math				
Lunch				
Social Studies				
Science				

Today I also had:

_____ PE _____ Library _____ Computer
_____ Art _____ Music _____ Speech
_____ OT _____ Resource

Other Special Event:_____

Teacher Comment:

_____

_____

Parent Comment:

_____

_____

_____

Notes

1001 Great Ideas for Teaching and Raising Children with Autism or Asperger's, Revised and Expanded 2nd Edition
by Ellen Notbohm and Veronica Zysk
ISBN: 9781935274063

Answers to Questions Teachers Ask about Sensory Integration: Forms, Checklists, and Practical Tools
by Carol Kranowitz and Stacey Szklut
ISBN: 9781932565461

Basic Skills Checklists: Teacher-friendly Assessment for Students with Autism or Special Needs
by Marlene Breitenbach
ISBN: 9781932565751

The CAT-kit: The new Cognitive Affective Training program for improving communication!
by Tony Attwood, Kirsten Callesen, and Annette Moller Nielson
ISBN: 9781932565737

Building Bridges through Sensory Integration: Therapy for Children with Autism and Other Pervasive Developmental Disorders
by Paula Aquilla and Shirley Sutton
ISBN: 9781932565454

How Do I Teach This Kid?: Visual Work Tasks for Beginning Learners on the Autism Spectrum
by Kimberly Henry
ISBN: 9781932565249

Inclusive Programming for Elementary Students with Autism
by Sheila Wagner
ISBN: 9781885477545

Inclusive Programming for High School Students with Autism or Asperger's Syndrome
by Sheila Wagner
ISBN: 9781932565577

Inclusive Programming for Middle School Students with Autism or Asperger's Syndrome
by Sheila Wagner
ISBN: 9781885477842

Learning in Motion: 101+ Sensory Activities for the Classroom
by Patricia Angermeier and Joan Krzyzanowski
ISBN: 9781932565904

My Friend with Autism: A Children's Book for Peers
by Beverly Bishop and Craig Bishop
ISBN: 9781885477897

The New Social Story Book, Revised and Expanded 10th Anniversary Edition: Over 150 Social Stories that Teach Everyday Social Skills to Children with Autism or Asperger's Syndrome, and Their Peers
by Carol Gray
ISBN: 9781935274056

No More Meltdowns: Positive Strategies for Managing and Preventing Out-of-Control Behavior
by Jed Baker
ISBN: 9781932565621

Sensitive Sam: Sam's Sensory Adventure Has a Happy Ending!
by Marla Roth-Fisch
ISBN: 9781932565867

Squirmy Wormy: How I Learned to Help Myself
by Lynda Farrington Wilson
ISBN: 9781935567189

The Social Skills Picture Book: Teaching Play, Emotion, and Communication to Children with Autism
by Jed Baker
ISBN: 9781885477910

Ten Things Every Child with Autism Wishes You Knew
by Ellen Notbohm
ISBN: 9781932565300

Ten Things Your Student with Autism Wishes You Knew
by Ellen Notbohm
ISBN: 9781932565362

A Treasure Chest of Behavioral Strategies for Individuals with Autism
by Beth Fouse and Maria Wheeler
ISBN: 9781885477361

Ultimate Guide to Sensory Processing Disorder: Easy, Everyday Solutions to Sensory Challenges
by Roya Ostovar
ISBN: 9781935274070

Understanding Asperger's Syndrome, Fast Facts: A Guide for Teachers and Educators to Address the Needs of the Student
by Emily Burrows and Sheila Wagner
ISBN: 9781932565157

All resources are available in bookstores everywhere, Amazon.com, and on the publisher's website www.FHautism.com.

Beth Aune, OTR/L currently has a private practice as a pediatric occupational therapist in the Coachella Valley area. She and her dedicated staff provide intervention for children with autism spectrum disorder, developmental disabilities, and other diagnoses in a variety of environments: early  intervention in the home, for general and special education students in the school setting, and in the clinical setting. Beth has developed and presented numerous workshops and trainings for parents and educators that focus on the care and treatment of children with disabilities. She is passionate about her profession as an occupational therapist and considers it a calling. She lives in Palm Desert with her three children.

Beth Burt currently resides in Southern California with her husband, their two sons, two cats and a dog. Because of her experience with her own children, one with an autism spectrum disorder (ASD) and the other with a learning disability, she  became an advocate. She has over thirteen years of experience collaborating and advocating on behalf of students with ASD and other disorders. She has been actively involved in numerous task forces and committees related to children, disabilities, and education. She has presented numerous times in Southern California to colleges, conferences, parent groups, and businesses. She is currently President of the Inland Empire Autism Society and is a board member of the Autism Society of California and Visions R Us, a nonprofit organization that assists young adults with special needs in making the transition from high school to desired employment.

Peter Gennaro is currently the Director of Special Education for the Alvord Unified School District in Southern California. He served as Special Education Coordinator and as Program/Inclusion Specialist

prior to this. As a teacher, he taught classes for students with emotional disturbances and has taught direct service special education classes consisting of students with varying disabilities. In his current position he continues to work closely with teachers, service providers, and families to develop and implement successful student programs.

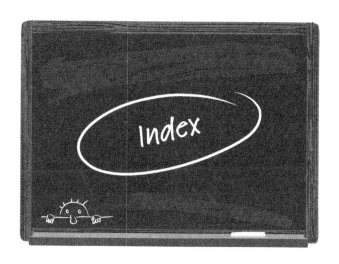

CPSIA information can be obtained at www.ICGtesting.com
Printed in the USA
BVOW06s0038040316

439035BV00003B/3/P

9 781935 274483